W9-BUJ-917

GREAT BARRIER REEF

Martin J. Gutnik
& Natalie Browne-Gutnik

Technical Consultant

Paul K. Dayton
Scripps Institution
of Oceanography

RSVP

RAINTREE STECK-VAUGHN
P U B L I S H E R S
The Steck-Vaughn Company

Austin, Texas

This book is in memory of Harold S. Browne and Max Gutnik

Copyright © 1995 by Raintree Steck-Vaughn Publishers.
All rights reserved. No part of the material protected by this copyright may be reproduced or utilized in any form or by any means, electronic or mechanical, including photocopying, recording, or by any information storage and retrieval system, without permission in writing from the copyright owner. Requests for permission to make copies of any part of the work should be mailed to: Copyright Permission, Raintree Steck-Vaughn Publishers, P.O. Box 26015, Austin, TX 78755

A production of B&B Publishing, Inc.

Editor – Jean B. Black
Photo Editor – Margie Benson
Computer Specialist – Katy O'Shea
Interior Design – Scott Davis

Raintree Steck-Vaughn Publishing Staff

Project Editor – Helene Resky
Project Manager – Joyce Spicer

LIBRARY OF CONGRESS CATALOGING-IN-PUBLICATION DATA

Gutnik, Martin J.
    Great Barrier Reef / Martin J. Gutnik, Natalie Browne-Gutnik
        p. cm. — (Wonders of the world)
    Includes bibliographical references and index.
    ISBN 0-8114-6369-9
    1. Coral reef biology — Australia — Great Barrier Reef (Qld.) — Juvenile literature. 2. Great Barrier Reef (Qld.) — Juvenile literature. [1. Coral reef biology. 2. Great Barrier Reef (Qld.)] I. Browne-Gutnik, Natalie.
II. Title. III. Series.
QH197.G85 1995
574.5'26367'09943 — dc20

94-3029
CIP
AC

Cover photo
The beauty of the Great Barrier Reef and its inhabitants

Title page photo
Sunlight brightens the reef at Heaven's Gate.

Table of Contents page photo
Clark's clownfish is one of the many fish to live in the Great Barrier Reef.

PHOTO SOURCES

Cover Photo: © Randall Sanders

Florida Marine Research Institute: 44 both

Great Barrier Reef Marine Park Authority: 12, 13 bottom, 14 bottom, 15, 16, 19 bottom, 29, 35 insets, 37 left margin, 38 top, 43, 54, 58, 60

© Al Grotell: 32

Carrol Henderson: 50 bottom, 51

Library of Congress: 4

National Aeronautics and Space Administration: 10

© Randall Sanders: 1, 3, 11, 14 top, 17 both, 18 both, 19 top, 20, 21 margin, 25 both, 26 top, 28, 30 both, 31 both, 33 both, 34, 35, 36, 37 right margin, 38 bottom, 39, 40, 41, 42 all, 46, 47 both, 48, 49, 50 margin, 53, 55 right margin, 57, 59 both

© Eugene Schulz: 5, 6, 26 bottom, 27, 52, 55 top

© Tom Till: 8-9, 23

Printed and bound in the United States of America.
  2 3 4 5 6 7 8 9 10 VH 99 98 97 96

Table of Contents

Chapter One

The Great South Land

A continent three times the size of North America! Geographers of the eighteenth century insisted there had to be such a continent in the Southern Hemisphere. It had to be there in order to balance the weight of Europe, Asia, and North America.

It was the 1760s, and King George III of England wanted to expand the British Empire beyond America. The discovery of this "Great South Land," undoubtedly filled with riches, was an enticing goal. It was one of the major reasons that the British Admiralty sent Captain James Cook on his voyages into the South Pacific.

James Cook, the son of a farm laborer in Yorkshire, England, was born in 1728. The farmer who employed James's father paid for the boy's schooling until James was 12, when he had to go to work. He discovered the sea as a teenager. He signed on as a ship's apprentice at 18 but continued to study math and astronomy. A self-educated man, his drive for success made him the leader of a major expedition into unexplored seas.

At the age of 26, Cook was offered command of his own ship. Instead, he joined the British Navy as an able seaman. He advanced rapidly through the ranks and, after two short years, was promoted to ship's master. His major talent was in creating detailed maps and charts of previously uncharted areas.

In addition to the quest for land, there was another important reason to explore the South Pacific. World scientists knew that on June 3, 1769, the planet Venus would pass between the Earth and the sun. This type of celestial event, called a transit, is very rare. It was important that the transit be observed from various points around the globe, so that scientists could use the various measurements they obtained to determine the Earth's distance from the sun.

Britain's Royal Society decided that the most advantageous place to observe the transit would be

"Here you may recapture a sense of wonder, unknown, perhaps since childhood . . . . All this beauty and inventiveness of design cannot necessarily be for mere survival. The object can scarcely be to enrapture tourists or provide islands for mutton birds to howl in. The whole thing baffles the mind."

— Elspeth Huxley in *The Great Barrier Reef*

Captain James Cook left England in 1768 for the Pacific Ocean and didn't return until 1771. During this voyage, he explored the east coast of Australia where he encountered the Great Barrier Reef.

This peaceful Australian beach along the Coral Sea *(right)* is protected by the Great Barrier Reef. The reef extends 1,200 miles (1,930 km) in the Coral Sea along the northeastern coast of Australia.

Captain Cook damaged his ship, HMS *Endeavour*, near this point on the reef which he called Cape Tribulation.

from the South Pacific. The society therefore persuaded George III to sponsor a voyage to the far side of the Earth.

The Royal Society chose James Cook to lead the expedition. Equipped with a full crew, scientific instruments, and scientists, Cook took charge of the HMS *Endeavour*, and set off to explore the seas and shorelines of this uncharted part of the world. After many months at sea, the *Endeavour* reached the eastern coast of Australia. Cook set out to explore the area and claim it for England.

On May 6, 1770, after spending several days anchored at its first landfall in Botany Bay in the south of Australia, the *Endeavour* threaded its way up the coast, so that Cook could chart the waters. Day after day, all he and his crew saw were numerous low islands and shadows of brightly colored shapes under the water. Suddenly, something hidden beneath the waters proved treacherous and punctured the *Endeavour*'s hull. Cook and his crew had grounded on the amazing coral structure that came to be known as the Great Barrier Reef.

Coral, Coral Everywhere

The Great Barrier Reef is considered by many people to be the eighth natural wonder of the world. Named by Matthew Flinders, an Australian explorer who served as commander of the British survey ship *Investigator*, the Great Barrier Reef is the longest coral structure in the world.

The reef consists of more than 2,500 individual reefs strung together, over a distance of about 1,200 miles (1,930 km). It begins slightly south of the Tropic of Capricorn (latitude 23° 30' south of the equator) and ends in the Torres Straits, just south of Papua, New Guinea. That's almost the distance from New York to Florida.

The reef covers an area of 80,000 square miles (207,200 sq km), or approximately the size of the state of Kansas, or of England and Scotland combined. In some places, the reef is as much as 45 miles (72 km) wide. In others, it apparently disappears altogether. Its distance from the mainland coast varies from 10 to over 100 miles (16.1 to 161 km).

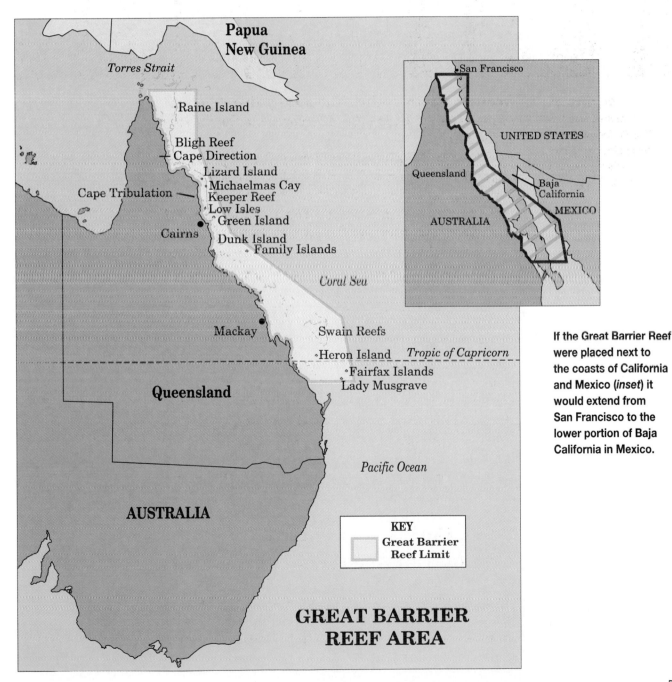

If the Great Barrier Reef were placed next to the coasts of California and Mexico (*inset*) it would extend from San Francisco to the lower portion of Baja California in Mexico.

GREAT BARRIER REEF AREA

KEY
Great Barrier Reef Limit

"... Everyone must be struck with astonishment, when he first beholds one of these vast rings of coral-rock, often many leagues in diameter, here and there surmounted by a low verdant island with dazzling white shores, bathed on the outside by the foaming breakers of the ocean, and on the inside surrounding a calm expanse of water, which, from reflection, is generally of a bright but pale green colour."

— Charles Darwin in *Structure and Distribution of Coral Reefs*

The Great Barrier Reef is the biggest structure ever constructed by living organisms. It is so big it can be seen from space. The reef was first fully mapped by the crew of Apollo 7 in October of 1968. The three-man crew was able to photograph the reef from space during their trip as they circled the Earth 163 times.

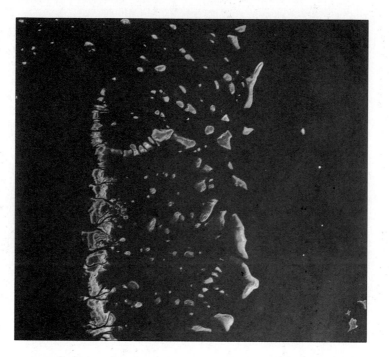

This section of the Great Barrier Reef was photographed from space. The area shown is 150 miles (241 km) east of the town of Mackay on the Australian mainland.

More than 200 years ago, the stranded Captain Cook viewed the reef from a more humble perspective. But even then, Captain Cook realized that he had stumbled upon one of the great natural phenomena of the world. After repairing and freeing his ship, he tried to chart the area near the Coral Sea. Today—even with the help of the astronauts—some of the islands remain uncharted and unexplored. In fact, many of the islands and reefs we see today probably did not exist when Cook and his crew were exploring.

The reef can be considered a kind of "super organism." The 2,500 reefs function together as one giant reef. What harms one part of it harms it all.

The reef consists largely of coral, a rocklike substance made by tiny animals, called polyps. These polyps, which exist in numbers too numerous to count, are constantly being born, reproducing, eating, dying, and—in the process—adding new coral to the reef. The reef is thus in a constant state of creation. In addition, the number of people who visit the reef cannot help but destroy parts of it. It would, therefore, have been impossible for Cook to anticipate what the Great Barrier Reef looks like today.

The rocky foundation of the Great Barrier Reef was built by hard, stonelike corals *(right)*. The hard material consists of outer skeletons, called exoskeletons, produced by tiny animals called coral polyps.

A professional underwater photographer captures the beauty of a feather starfish lodged on the reef.

Imagine that you are one of the crew on Cook's ship, as it lay caught on the reef. The sights you would see are quite beyond anything you've ever seen before. The colors are infinite and constantly changing with the angle of the sun. An object can be blue sometimes, red at other times. Orange is more orange than you can possibly describe. The pinks are rich and dramatic, while greens seem to be in the background everywhere.

You want to reach out and touch the colors, to convince yourself that they are real. Perhaps it's all a dream, but no dreamer could conjure up the variety of colors and shapes, the grace of movement, and the abundance of life on this living monument of coral.

You want to dive into the water and feel the

rocks that create this fantasy world. You want to be graceful like the fish and peaceful like the tentacles of the anemones undulating with the ocean current. You want to watch the drama of life unfold in this place that seems like another world.

Leather corals are neither soft nor hard but in-between.

Elspeth Huxley, a journalist, explored Australia, in 1965. Fascinated by the country and its people, she traversed the continent and wrote about every province and city. At Heron Island, she came upon the Great Barrier Reef. She wrote:

Here you may recapture a sense of wonder, unknown, perhaps since childhood. In a few square yards you can see a greater variety of shapes and patterns than the boldest artist could dream of, and there are thousands of square meters of this. No two ramifying branches, no two twigs, or cavities, or caves in miniature, or thumb-sized mountain ranges, are alike. And all this has been created by myriads of tiny polyps. Why, you ask, in heaven's name, why? All this beauty and inventiveness of design cannot necessarily be for mere survival. The object can scarcely be to enrapture tourists or provide islands for mutton birds to howl in. The whole thing baffles the mind.

Sea anemones attach themselves to the reef with tiny suction cups. They wait to strike unsuspecting prey with their poisonous tentacles. The anemone fish in the photo are swimming near the anemone's mouth, but the anemone will not harm them.

13

LIFE AND DEATH ON THE REEF

Many reef animals use poison to defend themselves or to attack other animals. The poisonous sting of the box jellyfish paralyzes prey instantly, including humans. The cone snail has tiny, sharp, poison-filled teeth that emerge from a hard shell to bite into an unsuspecting intruder. Innocent-looking catfish swim through the reef with deadly poison hidden in their fins. One of the reef's ugliest and most poisonous creatures is the stonefish. Its thirteen poisonous spines are so sharp and lethal that they can pierce rubber shoe soles and kill unsuspecting divers.

Some animals have developed interesting defense tactics. Tube worms (left) literally self-destruct if an attacker comes too close. Sea urchins are built for defense. Their sharp needlelike spines poison attackers, such as starfish. Starfish aren't good at defending themselves, but they do have the ability to simply regrow arms lost in battle.

Nature's Showplace

The variety of natural life is very apparent on the Great Barrier Reef. In few other places on Earth, perhaps only in the Amazon jungle, can nature's bounties and perils be found in such splendor. The reef itself, a maze of nooks and crannies, gardens of colors and caves, mountains, and flats, provides habitats for countless fish, plants, mollusks, and other forms of life. The diversity of life seems boundless, as does the knowledge that can be gained from observing this wondrous structure.

Taken individually the reef's creatures are wondrous, but it is their interrelationships that make them even more fascinating. Dr. Frank H. Talbot,

Mushroom coral is a common hard, building coral. Smaller tree fern corals surround the mushroom coral in the photo.

Soft corals, such as the ones in the photo, have internal spinelike skeletons. They attach themselves to the hard coral walls of the reef.

director of the Australian Museum, believes many of these interrelationships are so strange and complex that "they would make the largest computer in the world blanch." His statement was based on fact. Two computer experts and 40 biologists were hired by the Smithsonian Institution to create a computer simulation of the feeding relationships on the Great Barrier Reef. The computer was unable to do so.

The lessons that can be learned from observing this wondrous structure are undoubtedly endless. The reef has always grown and changed, naturally. But in the last thirty years, humans have brought unnatural change to this underwater wilderness. Simply by their presence, sports enthusiasts and tourists alter the environment they invade. Perhaps through education people will come to understand and appreciate this delicate wonder enough to protect its complicated web of life.

**This view is from
inside a coral cave
at Keeper Reef.**

Chapter Two

A Coral Reef

If you have ever held a piece of coral in your hands
and examined it, you may have seen intricate,
oddly shaped patterns on white rock. These patterns are made by tiny ridges of limestone, formed
into snowflake-shaped holes. Each one is different.
This network of limestone is known as a coral
colony. In the oceans of the world, coral colonies
form communities called coral reefs.

A coral reef is a garden of stone. But this garden
of stone is alive with activity. Most people, upon
first seeing a reef, are overwhelmed by all the colors
and varieties of life. Coral tentacles sway with the
ocean's currents. Fish swim in schools or individually, feeding on each other and the reef. Clams and
starfish cling to solid structures created by the
corals, feeding on living things that swim by, while
colorful nudibranches, or sea slugs, glide across the
rigid limestone.

It is this diversity of life on the reef that makes it so wonderful and fascinating. The coral reef is a tropical paradise in an ocean environment.

It is difficult for someone studying the reef to focus on any one aspect of this living ecosystem. Each species has its niche, or specific task, in the ecological functioning of the reef. There is no species or group that does not belong and does not have its own specific function—except, perhaps, humans.

One group of animals, however, is the basis of all life in the reef, the coelenterates, also called cnidarians. This group of animals includes hard coral, soft coral, sea fans, hydras, sea anemones, and many other animals. Many of the 350-plus species found in the Great Barrier Reef have not been named yet. All these animals play an important part in the functioning of the reef, but the corals, by far, contribute the most.

George Fichter, a writer specializing in aquatic subjects, says it all:

The appropriately named brain coral has a skeleton of almost pure calcium carbonate, more commonly known as limestone.

> . . . *The real reef formers are the hard or stony corals; their soft and jellylike bodies are surrounded by a hard, limy skeleton. Some forms look like trees or antlers; others appear as shrubby tubelike clusters; still others are squat masses resembling mushrooms. Some colonies are rocklike and reach weights of several tons; others are as light and delicate as crystal.*

The hard table corals build awesome flat coral structures.

Each individual coral animal is a polyp. These alcyone coral polyps are soft coral.

The Coral Polyp

Each individual coral animal is a polyp. It resembles the sea anemone and is often mistaken for this close relative. The polyp has the shape of a cup or a pouch. It can be as small as a period on this page or as large as a pea. Not until the 1700s did scientists recognize that coral polyps were animals and not nonliving objects.

The coral polyp is a carnivore, a flesh-eater. When a small, unsuspecting animal swims past the coral's tentacles, special cells in the tentacles sting it, usually rendering it unconscious. Then it can be devoured by the polyp.

Most corals hunt at night. During the day, they rest within their coral skeletons. After dark, they come out of their protective shelters and begin the hunt. Tentacles waving in the current, they search for food.

Some corals are solitary, but most are social creatures, building huge structures called colonies. In these colonies, thousands of corals are connected to one another by living tissue.

Living in colonies does not make corals remarkable. Forming huge communities of millions of corals does not make them remarkable either. What makes the coral polyps remarkable is their limestone-producing cells. These cells secrete limestone rock for their skeletons. The skeletons of billions of corals, laid down generation after gener-

The polyps of this mushroom coral sway in the warm, shallow water, looking for an evening meal.

HOW OLD IS THE REEF?

In 1990, Judith A. McKenzie, project co-chief of the Swiss Federal Institute of Technology, in Zurich, Switzerland, announced a dramatic new discovery. Geoscientists with the Ocean Drilling Program had recovered sediment cores from four areas on the slopes of the Great Barrier Reef, along Australia's northeastern shore. Using a technique called microfossil dating, they proved that the Australian part of the reef began forming some time between 500,000 and 1 million years ago. In terms of our Earth's geologic history, this makes the reef a baby.

ation, built the beautiful reefs that provide a habitat for thousands of marine species.

Formation of Coral Reefs

Corals are the great builders of the ocean. No other living organisms, including people, have constructed such vast and permanent structures. Even the Great Wall of China, one of the wonders of the human world, does not compare with the length, breadth, and architectural magnificence of the Great Barrier Reef.

A snorkler explores a shallow reef pool. At low tide, these portions of the reef may be exposed to the air and sunlight.

Parts of the reef
consist of huge coral
canyons, built over
hundreds of years.

Corals first appeared over 500 million years ago
and, since that time, they have created reefs in
most of the world's oceans. Today, reefs are found
mainly in tropical waters, between the Tropic of
Cancer, north of the equator, and the Tropic of
Capricorn, south of the equator. They thrive in the
warm waters of all oceans except where warm currents flow on the eastern shores of continents.
Reefs develop in shallow areas where the seafloor is
rocky or sandy.

There are many corals in polar seas, but they
are not the same kind of corals as those found on
the Great Barrier Reef. Cold water inhibits the formation of corals that grow with plants. Reefs also
will not grow in areas of ocean where freshwater
rivers get too muddy. This is why the northern end
of the Great Barrier Reef stops where it does—fresh
water from the rivers of New Guinea interferes with
the saltwater environment needed by the corals.

Types of Reefs

There are two main categories of reefs: oceanic and continental. The categories depend on the depth of the water in which the reefs are found.

Oceanic reefs are found far away from land, where the ocean floor rises in underwater mountain ranges. Some of these mountain ranges break the ocean's surface to form islands, and many reefs thrive in these shallow waters.

Atolls are oceanic reefs that circle a central lagoon. These reefs form in rings and appear suddenly from great ocean depths. The lagoons are usually very shallow, even though the water outside the atoll may be thousands of feet deep.

Continental reefs form close to non-reef landmasses. There are three types of continental reefs.

Shelf reefs form close to continents, on the sloping continental shelves. If the shelf has a hard bottom and is free of freshwater contamination, it provides the ideal environment for reef development.

Fringing reefs are shelf reefs that develop close to land in shallow water. No channel of water separates the reef and the shore. They arise from sea flats near the landmass or surrounding volcanic islands.

Barrier reefs are walls of coral that line the edge of a continental shelf. Barrier reefs separate the continental shelf from deep ocean waters. Off the coast of Australia, the Great Barrier Reef stands in water 325 to 650 feet (100 to 200 m) deep. However, on the seaward side of the reef, the ocean depth plunges to thousands of feet. A barrier reef usually encloses a lagoon with islands. The shallow, landward side of a barrier reef is generally colonized by fragile corals, while the seaward side is populated with hardy corals and certain algae. The Great Barrier Reef, in and of itself, is nothing more or less than a gigantic breakwater that protects the beautiful beaches of Queensland.

Atolls

How atolls form has been a subject debated for many decades. British scientist Charles Darwin, who explored much of the Southern Hemisphere, developed a theory of reef formation that still stands as the most likely explanation.

Darwin based his theory on the idea that the Earth's crust moves, an idea that was very controversial at that time. People were not yet ready to believe that the crust of the Earth moved and changed. This

Continental reefs are found all over the world. This one is in the Caribbean.

The edge of the Great Barrier Reef

idea seemed opposed to what they had learned from their religious leaders, who taught that the Earth was created by God to be perfect and was therefore unchanging.

Charles Darwin had already visited the Andes Mountains in South America when he first saw coral reefs in the Pacific Ocean. Having experienced an earthquake in the mountains, he started wondering whether when mountains rose in one area, the crust of the Earth sank, or subsided, in another. He then suggested that coral reefs, especially atolls, were the result of the crust under a volcano sinking slowly as the reef builders did their work up near the surface. Darwin wrote, "Under this view we must look at a lagoon island [an atoll] as a monument raised by myriads of tiny architects, to mark the spot where a former land lies buried in the depths of the ocean."

There was no way in the nineteenth century to prove or disprove Darwin's idea. It wasn't until the 1940s and 1950s that American scientists worked at Eniwetok in the Marshall Islands to prepare the island for a hydrogen bomb test. They drilled down into the island and discovered that a layer of coral-built limestone three quarters of a mile (1.2 km) thick covered volcanic rock 2 miles (3.2 km) thick. Darwin was right.

An atoll is a coral reef encircling a shallow body of water called a lagoon. Partially submerged reefs or small patches of sand called cays may lie within the reef.

He thought that land protruding from a tropical sea may develop a fringe of coral around it in shallow water. The land slowly sinks into the sea while the reef, through the growth of the coral, maintains its level in the water. Eventually the land disappears, and only the ring of coral—an atoll—remains.

The Great Barrier Reef, however, seems to defy Darwin's explanation of reef formation. The Great Barrier Reef is not just one reef but a series of different types of reefs, all lying in the very shallow waters off the continent of Australia.

The Wall of Coral

Many factors are involved in the formation of a coral reef. The limestone skeleton of each coral polyp is called a corallite. As the corals grow in colonies, the corallites join together in a corallum.

The polyps and corallites that make up a colony lose their individual identities. They become a mass of corallite ridges and valleys. The corallum is fused together by calciferous algae—a type of algae that secretes lime, which acts like a glue. The corallum forms a wall of life, an ecosystem that provides a home for other creatures of the ocean.

The corals, together with the other lime-secreting plants and animals, form a highly complex community that illustrates the many interrelationships in nature. Some organisms live independently, while others, like the corals, are totally dependent on other species for their survival. The lime-secreting algae hold the reef together, while other algae live inside the corals and provide them with nutrients and oxygen.

The Life Cycle of a Coral

The coral polyp, like most other forms of life, begins as a fertilized egg. The sperm and egg float to the surface and form an embryo. This fertilized egg releases a larva that floats and drifts with the watery currents. As it floats, the larva changes its shape and form many times. Sometimes it is a sliver of a disc, the next moment a pear-shaped droplet, and then a geyser-shaped fountain of clear, transparent tissue.

Finally, after ten days, or even many months, of floating and growing, the larva drops to a hard,

The Great Barrier Reef is composed of many separate reef structures. Each of these separate reefs has a different name.

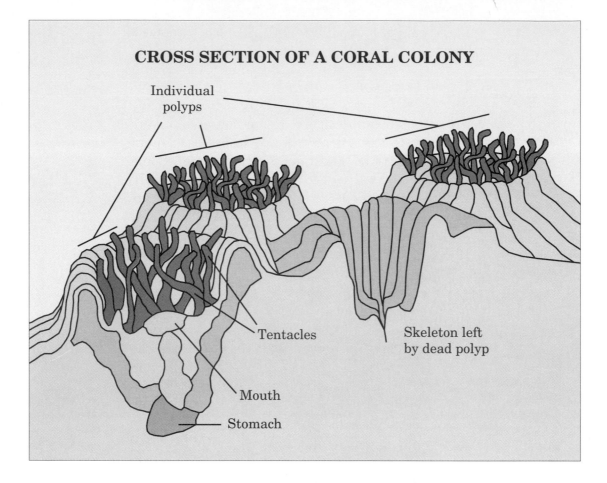

CROSS SECTION OF A CORAL COLONY

Individual polyps

Tentacles

Skeleton left by dead polyp

Mouth

Stomach

smooth surface on the reef, flattens itself, and immediately begins to secrete its white limestone skeleton. This skeleton will become its home, and here the polyp will live, grow, and reproduce for the rest of its life.

The polyp's body is transparent and filled with zooxanthellae, a type of algae that helps it take in oxygen and grow. These microscopic, one-celled algae spend their entire lives growing and reproducing within the tissues of the coral polyp.

By four weeks, the polyp's tentacles have developed. They extend from the main body of the polyp, often in an explosion of color. Within the tentacles are special cells that release deadly poison. The polyp excretes mucus, a thick, sticky, syruplike secretion, to attract unsuspecting prey. As an unwary animal is caught in the stickiness, it is stung and rendered helpless by the poison cells. Then it is passed to the mouth, located in the middle of the tentacles, where it is swallowed and digested.

Two Kinds of Reproduction

Reef building is an important part of the coral's life and a task that a single animal cannot accomplish. Through a process of reproduction called budding, corals produce vast numbers of exact copies of themselves, always connected to one another, all constantly producing limestone to build the reef.

Corals bud in many different ways, depending upon the species, but the end results are always the same—vast quantities of limestone forming a reef. Sometimes pieces of living coral, especially branching corals, are broken off and carried by the ocean currents to a different area. There, they may reattach themselves to a surface and start to build a whole new colony. This process gradually distributes reefs over a large area of the ocean floor.

Tubastra corals live in colonies where the polyps feed together at night. This photo shows the extended tentacles and mouth of a single tubastra polyp.

In reproducing by budding, each offspring is an exact duplicate of its parent—a clone. Budding is a form of asexual reproduction, meaning without males and females. Many corals also reproduce by sexual reproduction. One of the most important aspects of nature, especially in higher animals and plants, is the establishment of genetic variety and strength through the recombining of genes. Genes are material that pass on traits, such as strength, size, and color, from one generation to the next.

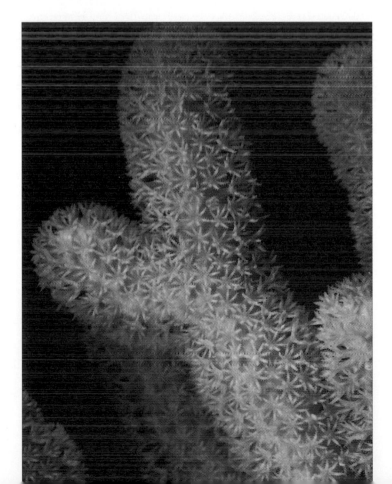

Octocorals are corals with non-poisonous tentacles having many branches, so that they appear feathery.

25

A green-finned parrot fish swims past limestone coral skeletons left behind when old polyps died.

In sexual reproduction, genes from males and females recombine in the offspring. In most corals, the egg and sperm develop in sacs within the tube-like body cavity of different animals and are then expelled through the open mouth. The egg is fertilized by the sperm, producing a larva called a planula. Once hatched, the planulae, which have hairs along their edges, drift with the currents as part of the plankton. Many of them are eaten, but some reach a hard, smooth surface, where they settle and start a new coral colony.

In the meantime, the original polyp may have died, since many reef corals have a life span of only one month. Once the original coral dies, it leaves behind its limestone skeleton, which becomes a permanent part of the rocky reef.

The Making of Islands

Sometimes, when a coral mass has grown too near the surface of the sea, it may begin to catch sand, weeds, and other ocean debris. Gradually, an island called a coral cay [pronounced *kee*] forms. Because many kinds of seeds are airborne, they may land on a cay and begin to grow. Eventually, as more and more plants die

This coral shoreline on Green Island was once part of an underwater reef. Sand and soil accumulated on top of the coral.

and decompose, soil is formed on top of the coral. Low cays may bear only grasses and a shrub or two. Others may develop a soil base deep enough to support whole forests of palms or trees.

Among the major types of trees that can grow on the coral cays is the banyan. The banyan is a wondrous tree. Its seed may lie in the branches of another tree or on top of a plant. When it germinates, aerial roots grow out of the seed and down to the soil, where they gradually establish themselves in the sand or soil. The roots slowly increase in thickness until a branch grows out sideways. Then new roots grow downward to support it. Those roots thicken, and the process continues. Ultimately, one plant can evolve into a tree more than 1,000 feet (300 m) wide.

Another unusual tree of the coral cay is the breadfruit tree. The name breadfruit originated because the starchy fruit of the tree, when baked, tastes like fresh bread. One variety of breadfruit, native to the South Sea Islands, is what Captain Bligh of the *Bounty* was transporting when his crew mutinied.

Mangrove trees send out aerial, or prop, roots that stabilize the tree in the waters along the shore of a coral cay.

This tree is unique in another way. Prop roots grow out from the trunk of the tree. The emerging roots have a cap on the end, which protects them until they grow into the ground. Over time, these roots surface from higher and higher up on the tree trunk, perhaps more than 7 feet (2 m) high.

The mangrove is the most common tree along Australia's east coast. Its prop roots look like the spine of an umbrella. When the aerial roots of one tree reach out for another, they join together to create an almost impenetrable barrier.

Sand catches among the roots of these trees, and gradually beaches form. The colorful displays of the corals and other reef life, in addition to the beaches, attract many tourists. Many of the tiny islands in the Caribbean Sea are coral cays.

Chapter Three

Life on the Reef

Millions of living creatures make their home on the Great Barrier Reef. Here, in an endless struggle for survival and the continuation of life, one can find all of the various interrelationships in nature.

As the coral mounds grow upward from the seabed, schools of shimmering fry, or young fish, move in unison from coral shoal to shoal, as they feast on microscopic plankton. They dance around a coral *bommie,* the Australian Aborigine name for a coral "head," a living mound of coral rising straight up to within a yard or two of the water's surface.

And death is always near, as large reef predators, colored to blend into their surroundings, lie in wait for unsuspecting prey. However, some predators, such as the blue-spotted coral trout and exquisite batfish, announce their presence to the world by a profusion of colors and forms.

Here among the coral crags other fish feed upon the reef itself. The chisel-toothed parrot fish breaks off pieces of limestone, in search of polyps, while angelfish dash in and gobble up the polyps from within their corallite skeletons.

A clown fish swims next to the reef while a school of young fish pass overhead.

"These stony remnants of the once living growths are frequently structures of beautiful and delicate design, and their diversity of shape and pattern is almost limitless. . . . Only a little imagination is required to picture these forms as crowded living growths covering large areas in many places along the great reef where ideal conditions prevail."

— Frank McNeill,
Curator at the
Australian Museum, in
*The Great Barrier Reef
and Adjacent Isles*

A large coral head, rising up from the seafloor, is called a coral *bommie.*

Farther out, away from the *bommie*, swim the fierce, open-water predators. Here, sharks, amberjacks, and barracudas lie in wait for stray fish. Then they strike quickly, make their kill, and vanish into the deep.

The crocodile fish blends in so well with the coral that it is almost impossible to see it.

Strange Shapes and Forms

Numerous animals, from corals to trumpet fish, live on the Great Barrier Reef. Many plants and animals are specifically adapted to this special environment. The scorpion fish, for example, inhabits the reef flats and looks like the rocks and sand beneath it. Camouflage also protects the stonefish, which lies motionless on the flats, looking like rough rock to its unsuspecting prey. The poison of the stonefish can be deadly even to humans. Each creature on the reef is specifically fitted for life in this coral forest.

From its elongated snout to its thin pencillike body, the trumpet fish seems a strange animal indeed. The trumpet fish often hitches a ride on other fish to conceal itself while moving about the reef in search of food.

The moray eel, its giant body hidden within the caverns in the reef, also conceals itself among the coral. Colored to blend in to the coral, it lies in wait. When an unsuspecting animal swims by, the eel attacks swiftly, doling out instant death with jaws strong enough to crush human bone.

The striped lionfish, with its winglike fins fluttering in the water, looks like an underwater angel dancing in the currents. But poison rests within those fins. The lionfish's spines can inflict a painful

Some moray eels grow to 10 feet (3 m) in length. This eel species is one of the largest predators in the reef system.

lesson to anything that attempts to bother it. Small lionfish are among the spectacular reef creatures often captured for saltwater aquariums.

Wide-eyed squirrelfish hide during the day in the crannies of the reef's underwater caves. At night they hunt in schools for protection.

Several of the most interesting and successful reef dwellers live among the branches of the coral reef. The red shrimp blends in perfectly with the vivid body of a sea urchin. It not only gains protection from staying close to the many writhing tentacles of the sea urchins, it also feeds off of it.

Crinoids have five or more feathery arms with a mouth in the middle. These creatures attach themselves to the coral wall.

The trigger fish uses an unusual form of adaptation called mimicry—looking like another living thing. The trigger fish hides among the sargassum seaweed community where it exactly mimics the color of the weeds, even to their dark shadow patterns. Predators mistake the trigger fish for the seaweed and pass by. The fish remains safe and undisturbed.

The lionfish has sharply contrasting markings that warn predators against attack. Each of its long spines contains deadly poison.

Sea slugs, also known as nudibranches, come in a variety of colors, from reds to oranges and yellows. These bright little creatures are fearless as they browse the ridges of coral. Like many other reef animals, they are very poisonous and therefore safe from predators.

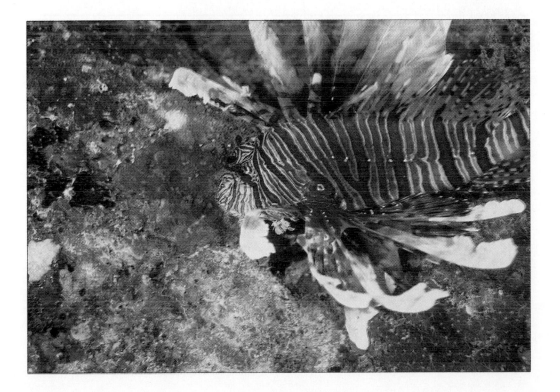

Plants of the Reef

The food chain on the reef begins with plants. Green plants, whether on land or in water, are the primary producers of food for themselves and for all other living things, because only green plants can produce food.

The plants of the coral reef not only make food, they also cement the reef together. Without the limestone cement provided by certain algae, the reef would not be as strong as it is.

Most of the algae on the reef are hidden within the transparent tissues of the corals. These tiny, one-celled plants carry on the process of photosynthesis in the tissues of these living animals. There are billions of these algae. Because they live within the tissues of an animal, they are referred to as zooxanthellae. However, these algae often leave the coral's body cavity to swim freely in the water and absorb sunlight.

Calcareous red algae produce limestone just as the stonelike corals do.

Other very abundant plants include calcareous red algae. This alga is responsible for laying down limestone, just as the corals do. Because it is very strong and resistant to battering, most of this type of algae is found on the seaward side of the reef, where the reef takes a pounding from the surf.

Other plants on the reef do not exist in large numbers, because they are eaten almost as fast as they can grow. Among these plants are seaweed and fleshy green algae.

A parrot fish searches for hard coral to eat with its hard, beaklike mouth. When the fish bite into coral, the sound is so loud it can be heard from a distance away.

Up the Food Chain Ladder

The second step in the reef's food chain is occupied by animals that eat only plants. These animals are called herbivores. Many of the worms on the reef are herbivores. Some herbivores burrow into the reef itself. Here they wait in their tiny caves for food to float by them. The colorful surgeonfish is an herbivore that feeds in the shallow areas of the reef. Sea urchins graze the reef by scraping bits of algae from the rock with their mouths, which are located on the underside of their bodies.

Herbivores are, in turn, eaten by carnivores, or flesh-eaters. Some carnivores eat only herbivores, and others eat other carnivores. Life on the reef is so complex and rich in variety that carnivores find a choice buffet of tidbits. Many carnivores eat something different each day. The long fin banner fish is a butterfly fish that feeds on a variety of invertebrates, such as mollusks, anemones, oysters, and clams, which it finds within the crevices of the reef. The Venus stickfish must work hard for its prey. It fans away sand with its fins to get at worms and crustaceans that the movement exposes.

Sometimes sea urchins use their powerful mouths to chisel through hard coral skeletons, digging out plant material inside.

Many animals on or near the reef are litter feeders who eat the organic material that swims or floats to the surface. This group includes many mollusks and the graceful manta ray, or devilfish. The manta ray swims close to the surface, filtering large amounts of soft floating animals into its mouth.

The barracuda, a sleek, swift predator, feeds on the larger carnivores in the open waters around the reef. After it strikes, it escapes with its prey into the shadowless deep. The barracuda is sometimes called the "tiger of the sea" because of its viciousness.

Barracudas have rows of sharp teeth that kill prey very quickly. They swim in the open sea beyond the reef edge.

The intense struggle for survival is a daily routine on the Great Barrier Reef. This is especially evident when one notices all of the creatures that feed upon the reef builders themselves. These animals are omnivores—they eat both flesh and plant material.

The elephant trunked cone shell carries a barbed, venomous dart and feeds on corals, as does the wentletrap. The parrot fish and the crown-of-thorns starfish also eat the corals. The crown-of-thorns starfish is a poison-spined coral predator, with an infamous reputation. It inverts its stomach over a colony of corals and digests them by absorbing the polyps directly into its system. In the early 1960s, large numbers of the crown-of-thorns starfish appeared on the Great Barrier Reef and began to literally destroy the reef by sucking the living corals out of their skeletons.

According to Dr. Robert Endean, of the University of Queensland, large areas covering hundreds of miles of reef have been ruined by these fish. Most scientists believe the crown-of-thorns starfish infestation was cyclical—a regular event that occurs periodically—but Dr. Endean does not agree with this theory. He thinks the crown-of-thorns starfish infestation was triggered by some unknown phenomenon.

The balance of nature prevents these animals from destroying the reef. Only when people intervene does this balance get disturbed—and then the reef is endangered.

The crown-of-thorns starfish feeds on hard coral, such as staghorn *(right)*, by inverting its stomach over the coral. In the early 1960s, large areas of the reef were completely stripped of coral by these starfish. The picture on the top left shows a portion of the reef before a crown-of-thorns invasion. The one on the bottom right shows the destruction of the reef afterward.

Partnerships on the Reef

Within the reef's rich and varied life, there are some remarkable associations between different species. Life on the reef is difficult at best, so some plants and animals, in order to survive, form close, life-giving relationships with other species.

The reef itself is a gigantic partnership of 2,500 reefs strung together, with over 500 islands and 500 fringing reefs. Within this giant system, partnerships exist inside each coral polyp. The zooxanthellae algae live in the soft tissue of the polyp and carry on the process of photosynthesis, producing glucose for food and oxygen. The coral polyp uses some of the glucose and the oxygen to carry on its life functions. The algae, in turn, receive protection and a supply of carbon dioxide—a gas necessary for photosynthesis—from the polyp. In this way, both corals and algae flourish in the tropical waters.

The male and female damselfish have a unique cooperative relationship. The male cleans an area of dead coral before he performs a special dance to entice the female. After she lays the eggs, he fertil-

Divers feeding a potato cod and moray eel are not part of the usual partnerships on the reef.

36

izes them and continues to watch over the eggs until they hatch four days later.

The clown fish and the striped damselfish dance in and out of the tentacles of the deadly sea anemones. They seem to be immune to the poisonous sting of the sea anemone, which kills other smaller fish. These fish are protected from predators by the presence of the anemone, and the anemone receives bits of food left over from the fish's meal. Sometimes the fish will actually place food within in the anemone's tentacles.

The coral crab scuttles along the reef and carries a tiny sea anemone within its claws. The crab eats nutritious matter produced by the anemone's body. The anemone, besides getting a free ride, gets bits of food from the crab's other meals.

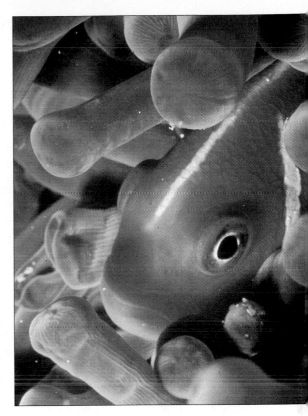

The tiny cleaner wrasse is like the dentist that makes house calls. It swims into the mouth of a larger fish, such as a barracuda or coral trout, and picks food particles from between the predator's daggerlike teeth. The large fish only has to open its mouth and let the wrasse do its work. The wrasses may also pick bits of torn skin off the larger fish.

There are many other tiny species of fish and shrimp that survive in this same manner. Busy all the time, they swim in and out of the mouths of eels, manta rays, rock cod, and other large predators, giving them their routine cleaning. The tiny cleaners benefit by getting their food supply from the large carnivores. The carnivores benefit by being kept clean of bits of food, parasites, bacteria, and fungal infections.

The largest clam in the world, the *Tridacna gigas*, inhabits the Great Barrier Reef. Estimates of the weight of these animals vary from 200 to 500 pounds (91 to 227 kg), with a diameter of 3 to 4 feet (.9 to 1.2 m). According to local folklore, people have drowned when they accidentally walked into an open clamshell and became trapped when the valves, or shell halves, closed upon the trespasser.

The clam has a relationship with the algae zooxanthellae, similar to that of the cleaner wrasse and the barracuda. Through the process of photosynthesis, the algae produce carbohydrates, which

A clown fish waits in the tentacles of an anemone for prey to pass by. For some unknown reason, anemones do not attack such hiding clown fish.

Giant clams are still found in the Great Barrier Reef. However, poachers from as far away as Taiwan come to Australia and illegally strip clams from the outlying reefs.

REEF FISHING

Imagine catching a fish that weighs 1,000 pounds (454 kg)! Lizard Island, 150 miles (242 km) north of the reef capital of Cairns, in North Queensland, is famous for its black marlin. From September through November, anglers may be lucky enough to see schools of ten or more black marlin, each weighing between 150 and 1,000 pounds (68 and 454 kg). Don't bother bringing your ultralight tackle. Serious anglers use 130-pound (60-kg) test line.

For bait, they use a little fish that averages less than one pound (0.45 kg). Called a queenfish, it is commonly referred to as a queenie. Queenies are a natural bait, very tough and resilient. The marlin school near the reef openings. Just visu-alize catching a "grander"—the term Australian anglers use for the 1,000-pounders—with a one-pound bait!

However, don't plan on eating your trophy. The big ones have to have tags put on them and are then released. With this tag-and-release pro-gram, scientists are able to monitor the migratory patterns of these mega-fish.

Not all fishing is for such game as the giant black marlin or sailfish. Some people use handlines to fish the bottom of a reef. Often an angler will pull up a coral trout, red emperor, or Spanish mackerel. Spearfishing from charter boats is also growing in popularity, but spearfishing with scuba is illegal.

are absorbed by the clam. The clam's waste products then become nourishment for the algae.

There are also partnerships in which one of the partners benefits, while the other is neither helped nor harmed. Such partnerships are called commensal relationships. The trumpet fish steals a ride on a larger predator, perhaps a coral trout or rock cod. The large predator eats only large prey, so it ignores the little trumpet fish, as well as any other small fish that swim by. However, the trumpet fish darts off its companion's back and gobbles up the smaller fish. The trumpet fish benefits by being able to get close enough to capture its prey. The larger predator is neither helped nor harmed—and probably doesn't even notice the intrusion of the trumpet fish.

The coral trout is one of the largest predatory fish on the reef.

The pilot fish accompanies many sharks and shares a similar relationship with these fearsome predators of the deep. As a shark rips its prey into bite-sized chunks, many loose pieces of flesh are released into the water. The pilot fish capture these tasty morsels and devour them. They benefit from this relationship, while the shark is neither helped nor harmed.

The remora, also called a shark sucker, attaches itself to

the shark by means of a sucker on its head. The fish gets a free ride from the shark as well as protection from predators. In turn, the remora cleans parasites from the shark's body. The relationship between the shark and remora is mutualistic, while the one with the pilot fish is commensal.

The blenny is a mimic of the cleaner fish. Being almost exactly like the cleaner fish in color and action, the blenny fools a larger fish into believing it is about to receive a cleaning. Instead, this tricky little fish gets into the larger fish's gill and bites a lump of living tissue. The blenny is a parasite, living off its host, the larger fish. This kind of relationship is called parasitism. The blenny benefits, while the host fish is harmed.

Dr. Walter Starck, a marine biologist, discovered a very unusual relationship. Four species rely on the anemone for food and shelter. However, parasites attached to the fish are attracted by the anemone tentacles and become food for one of the protected shrimp species. Though Dr. Starck refers to this as a four-way relationship, the last relationship actually makes it a six-way relationship.

Tiny shrimp exploit their hosts for food, either by stealing it, by letting the host partially digest it, or by feeding on the host's flesh itself.

Among the many fascinating aspects of reef life, I think are the close relationships among different animals. . . . I discovered one cleaner shrimp, astonishingly enough, to be a member of a four-party relationship. It lives in the shelter of a sea anemone's stinging tentacles. The shrimp Periclimenes pedersoni attracts fish toward the anemone with its long, waving antennae, then darts out of hiding to feed on the visitor's parasitic crustaceans and worms. We had known this three-way relationship, but the fourth party did not reveal itself until I interfered, by touching one anemone. . . . A husky little snapping shrimp emerged from beneath the anemone and thumped my finger with its outsize snapping claw. By living within the shelter of the sea anemone's tentacles, the snapping shrimp also enjoys protection.

There are endless examples of relationships among the reef's creatures. The Great Barrier Reef can be a school for a lifetime of study.

Chapter Four

The Rhythms on the Reef

The sun begins to set over the western coast of Australia, and life starts to change on the reef. With the dimming of the daylight, the pace of the living creatures seems to quicken in a host of activities.

Fish and many other reef dwellers move from their daytime niches to their nighttime niches. Gardens of coral seem to sway back and forth amid the frenzied activity. Some species of fish come out of their hiding places, while others vanish. Each creature that is active during the day attempts to find a safe resting place for the night. And the reef comes alive as its nighttime workers awaken after sleeping all day.

Accompanying the subtle change in light intensity, as the transition from day to night continues, comes the even more subtle change in the coloration of many of the reef's species. Animal coloration is highly adaptive and often changes with the animal's

"While the scene by daylight may be as rich and satisfying a sight as a visitor desires, it cannot match the wonders that are revealed when darkness falls."

— Frank McNeill, Curator at the Australian Museum, writing in The Great Barrier Reef and Adjacent Isles

A large, branching coral stands guard on a reef wall as day darkens into night. Life on the reef enters a new active phase when the sun goes down.

environment. Coloration is almost always protective in nature. It enables the smaller and defenseless creatures to hide from the large predators. The predators, however, also use coloration in order to conceal themselves, as they lie in wait to snatch an unwilling meal.

Schools of fish hurry to find protection in the nooks and crannies of the reef as the transition begins. Strays who separate from the school are in danger as the large predators, such as the barracuda and trout, go after lone fish.

As the amount of daylight decreases, each species seems to blend in perfectly with the surroundings. All the tricks of protective coloration are employed by species trying to avoid the large predators and find a safe spot for the night. The

A school of coral catfish swim in tight formation. Although they look harmless, they have poison in their fins.

During the day, mushroom coral polyps are contracted *(inset)*. At night the polyps extend their tentacles to feed *(left)*.

bright colors of many daytime fish are muted at sundown. This makes them less visible in the shadows and crannies of the reef.

Using mimicry—a technique of camouflage, in which an animal or plant imitates what another species looks like—the triggerfish can completely hide itself in a sargassum weed community. The bright colors and shadow patterns of the triggerfish almost exactly repeat the colors and design of the sargassum weed.

The parrot fish, a daytime feeder, finds a hidden crevice and surrounds itself with a self-made mucus sac. It will spend the night within this sac, hidden from its enemies.

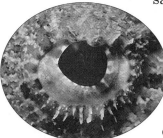

Every creature must be alert to danger as day becomes night. This scorpion fish watches intently for any sign of trouble.

As the sun sinks toward the horizon, the corals themselves begin to change. During the day, the corals are inactive, their food-seeking tentacles withdrawn and curled. As night approaches, these tiny creatures become alive with activity.

When the sun is almost gone from the sky, the varied colors of the reef shift in intensity and hue. The reef becomes still after what was a hustle of activity just moments before. Most movement ceases, and the reef and its many inhabitants enter a transitional quiet period.

Sunset is the most dangerous time for many of the reef inhabitants. It is twilight. The daytime inhabitants are safe in their hiding places, and the nighttime fish have not yet emerged.

Some fish, confused by the transition, have not yet found a resting place. Their eyes and other light-receiving structures fail them in the shadow of dusk, and they are extremely vulnerable. As they wait helplessly for their senses to adjust, a lurking predator can find easy prey.

Others find safety in the twilight. The fusilier fish sleeps, its natural red color subdued and broken by splotches and shadows, allowing the fish to blend into its surroundings. Other animals find protected resting places in the chinks and cavities of the reef.

All species, including people and coral reef creatures, are sensitive and responsive to both daily and yearly cycles. Their biological clocks regulate almost all their major functions, depending upon the amount of light.

Green sea turtles lay their eggs at night on the beaches of Green Island and Raine Island between October and February each year.

Sea Turtles at Night

Six of the seven major species of sea turtles come to lay their eggs in the coral isles. Green Island and Raine Island are frequented by green turtles, the most numerous of all the sea turtles. Another species—the hawksbill—produces a valuable tortoise shell often used in ornaments, especially by the Japanese. Because of its valuable shell, the

Tiny turtle hatchlings quickly head for the sea. Their soft shells make them very vulnerable prey.

hawksbill has been heavily hunted and has become very rare. It is now protected by international agreements. Another turtle, the loggerhead, is a meat-eater. It may have a body six feet long.

A mature green sea turtle female—one who is at least 50 years old—mates with at least four males and stores enough sperm to fertilize her eggs. Then, at high tide from October to February, visitors to the islands might hear a rhythmic, heaving, swishing-brushing sound in the night. It is made by the sea turtle females shuffling their cumbersome bodies out of the water to lay their eggs on the sands.

Using her long front flippers, each giant creature scrapes out a crater in the sand. Then she uses her shorter, agile hind flippers to dig a narrow, deep shaft down into the damp sand. Quietly perched over the hole, the turtle lays round, white eggs that look like ping-pong balls. After covering them with sand, she trundles back to the water. She usually lays about 100 eggs each night, fertilizing them as she deposits them in the nest. She will return to the beach every two weeks until she has laid approximately 1,000 eggs in different spots.

Each female green sea turtle lays between 50 and 200 round, spongy eggs on each visit to the sandy beach of an island.

The eggs hatch after about nine weeks, always at night. The young turtles, called hatchlings, instinctively dig up through the deep sand and make a beeline—or a "turtleline"—for the sea. This is the most dangerous time of their lives. Their shells are still soft, and they make good eating for seabirds, land predators, and fish.

The hatchlings that make it to the water instantly seek shelter on the bottom. Like most sea creatures, sea turtles are protected by a form of camouflage. They are dark on top and pale underneath. This protective arrangement of colors is called countershading.

The lives of young turtles are very precarious. Until their shells harden, they are still easy prey and are subject to being eaten. The odds against the survival of young sea turtles are very high. Only one sea turtle in 5,000 that hatches lives to reach maturity and produce its own offspring.

Living things respond differently as nighttime descends on the reef.

Night on the Reef

Darkness finally closes in, and the regular nighttime pattern of the reef emerges. Creatures that have slept for the entire day wake again, and the reef begins to bustle with activity. Sea slugs, starfish, crabs, worms, and hundreds of other species emerge from their daytime hiding places and carry on the activities of their lives under cover of darkness.

The most dramatic change on the reef at night occurs within the corals. During the day, their tentacles remain contracted, but at night their feathery arms unfurl. They catch zooplankton and direct the tiny animals into their mouths. They will keep busy eating until dawn.

As the sun sets, the corals sense that the light is gone. How the polyps sense the absence of light is

Daisy coral is called a leathery coral—it is neither soft nor hard. At night its polyps expand like a bouquet of daisies.

not known. Perhaps there are light receptors in their tentacles. Some scientists believe the polyp senses that the photosynthesis by the algae within the polyp's body has slowed, and, therefore, there is an absence of light. But if this were the case, why do some corals that don't have that photosynthesizing algae also unfurl at night? How do these corals sense the absence of light? Why is their response to light so rapid? When a diver abruptly shines a light on any of these nonphotosynthesizing corals, they retract their tentacles within a few seconds. Maybe researchers will be able to tell us why some day.

The zooplankton, too, respond to the absence of light. By day, millions of these tiny floating creatures, such as crustaceans and larvae, hide in the crevices of the reef. As the sun disappears over the western rim, they emerge, rising to the surface. At this time, many are trapped in the tentacles of the coral polyps and become an evening meal. Perhaps the corals have evolved to open at night because of the movement of the zooplankton.

In the dark, the limestone avenues of the reef become crowded with nighttime traffic. Moray eels slither across the seafloor in search of food, and coral shrimp comb the rocks and crevices. Sea urchins, shy by day, roam the seafloor, looking for a meal.

Feather stars—an ancient group of animals relat-

Crinoids, on sea lilies (*left*), stand out like flowers on the hard rock of the reef. Crinoids are related to starfish.

Adult nudibranches— also known as sea slugs—are mollusks without shells. Decorated with vibrant colors, they need the cover of night to protect them while they graze on the reef.

ed to the starfish and sea urchins—also hunt the drifting plankton. Creating a rainbow of colors, they spread their silken arms in search of prey. Like the coral, they filter the prey to a central mouth, where the tiny creatures are swallowed and digested.

Sea fans also come out at night, perching themselves on a protruding lump of coral about six feet above the seafloor. As the plankton rise from the bottom, the sea fans capture a meal in their downward-facing mouths.

Even under a starless sky, the reef itself will never appear dark. Sparks of light flash green, as if the water were filled with millions of fireflies. The sparks, caused by phosphorescent plankton that are invisible by day, are swept by the current in an eerie dance. The light show is the result of chemical changes that occur in plankton when they are disturbed by the movements of the water.

Night wears on, and the activity on the reef continues nonstop. Finally, as the sun edges up to the eastern rim of the sea, daybreak comes to the reef. As at dusk, the reef enters another period of quiet transition.

As the eastern sky colors, the nocturnal fish seek out their daytime hiding places among the reef's jagged edges. At the same time, the daytime fish and other creatures begin to emerge. The tentacles of the corals retract into their corallite skeletons to rest while the algae carry on photosynthesizing during the daytime hours. Finally, the parrot fish sheds the safety of its mucus cocoon and begins to feed on the sleeping corals.

Another day has come to the reef. Its rhythms and cycles continue the never-ending process of life.

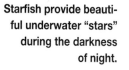

Starfish provide beautiful underwater "stars" during the darkness of night.

The Rhythm of the Tides

Tides moving in and out among the coral islands and reef beds create a different kind of daily rhythm. The color of the water changes as the tides move in and out, covering and exposing various regions of the reef.

An elegant fan coral provides a beautiful setting for this feather starfish *(right)*. This starfish has arms with a feathery fringe. Sometimes starfish feed as they drift along, attached to moving objects.

Coral must be particularly hardy to survive the daily drying that the receding tide brings to the upper parts of the reef. However, smaller corals remain safe in the depressions of the coral rock that catch water as the tide goes out.

The Rhythm of the Year

About 90 percent of the Great Barrier Reef is always underwater. There are, however, some areas of permanently dry land. These dry spots serve as nesting grounds for sea turtles and birds. During breeding season, the turtles swim in from the sea, and the birds fly in from the vast ocean.

Seabirds nest on the low sandy beaches of the reef's islands.

During the same months when turtles lay their eggs, numerous seabirds congregate on the dry parts of the reef to lay their eggs as well. Herons, terns, tropic birds, gannets, and frigate birds, among others, are drawn to the islets and cays of the reef by the abundance of food. There are thousands, perhaps millions, of sand-filled depressions that make attractive nesting sites.

Raine Island is the most important nesting island in Australia, for both sea turtles and terns. More than 100,000 terns nest there. Can you imagine 100,000 birds as they swoop around, chirping, cackling, and screeching at the same time?

During the nesting season, not all is idyllic. The silver gull lies in wait for eggs to be left untended, so it can gulp them down. Avid scavengers, gulls leave few animals of the reef alone when they are hungry.

Just north of Green Island lies Michaelmas Cay. Its low sandy beaches make an ideal nesting area for the sooty tern. During the day, the terns leave their nests and go out to sea to catch squid and small fish to feed their young. On the way back, their crops loaded with food, they often encounter a bird called the

MASTER OF THE SKIES

If you saw a frigate bird on land, you'd never know what an expert flier it is. On land these birds are awkward travelers; the skies are their home. With a powerful wingspan of approximately 7 feet (2.1 m), frigate birds soar and glide effortlessly above the reef. Although boobies and gannets are very good fliers, no bird species tops the frigate bird. Occasionally frigate birds interrupt a flight to get food, often catching fish dropped by other seabirds in midair. They also skim quickly along the water's surface, darting into the water to catch fish. Frigate birds spend time on the ground only during breeding season, when the nest must be tended. Both the male and female birds incubate the egg. Any other time of the year frigate birds take flight at dawn and don't return to the reef until dark.

Masked boobies are among the fastest flying seabirds on the reef.

frigate bird. It flies at the terns, surprising them and causing them to drop the food. When this happens, the thieving frigate bird swoops down and grabs the food in mid-air.

South of Green Island, gannets nest for the summer on Fairfax Island and Lady Musgrave Island. Here, one can look to the skies and see the red-backed sea eagle soaring. Sea eagles eat carrion—dead or decaying material. For hours, these birds float in the air currents above the beaches, looking for food.

Heron Island, named for the many white herons who migrate here between October and April, is also home to the muttonbird. These birds skim the surface of the water and build nests in burrows. There is a legend that the first European sailors fled from Heron Island, certain it was haunted. In fact, what they heard was the ghostly howling of these muttonbirds in their nightly courtship.

All life is subject to the cycles and rhythms of the sun. Although the Great Barrier Reef itself seems unchanging, life within it varies from day to night, from tide to tide, from season to season, and from year to year. It is a place of continuous change.

Chapter Five

Will There Be A Tomorrow?

The coast of Queensland has many beautiful untouched beaches and dense rain forests. The scenery is much the same as it was when the first people came to Australia.

Geologists say that a land bridge once connected Queensland and New Guinea. Over this bridge the original people, the ancestors of Australia's Aborigines, traveled to the continent.

The Aborigines have populated Queensland for at least 20,000 years. They explored the Great Barrier Reef in their canoes. Among the reef's islands and passages, they hunted sharks, mullet, shellfish, and sea turtles.

Ancient maps and charts show that the Chinese and Japanese were in what is now Queensland between 400 and 1,000 years ago. Portuguese navigators explored the area in the early 1500s.

The coming of the Europeans brought trouble and change to the Aborigines' way of life. The Europeans made war with the Aboriginal tribes and killed the people, reducing their population to a fraction of its original size. Many of the defeated people were made slaves.

Exploring the Reef

Starting with Captain James Cook, arriving in 1770 on the *Endeavour,* many Europeans have been captivated by Queensland and the Great Barrier Reef. More than 500 ships have sunk in the treacherous currents near the reef when their captains tried to satisfy their curiosity.

Sir Joseph Banks, a British naturalist who sailed with Captain Cook, was the first scientist to view the coral reef. Edmund Halley, a mathematician and astronomer royal of Great Britain, also came in the 1700s. Halley is best known for predicting the passage of a comet which has come to bear his name—Halley's Comet.

The infamous English commander of the ship *Bounty,* Vice Admiral William Bligh, visited the Great Barrier Reef in 1789. He found a way through the reef at a spot known as Bligh Reef Island, near Cape Direction. Soon after his visit the first merchant ship came through. English naturalist Charles Darwin, English biologist Thomas Henry Huxley, and American zoologist Alexander Agassiz arrived in the 1800s.

In 1798, English naval captain Matthew Flinders was the first of many to explore the coast of the Great Barrier Reef. His detailed charts are the foundation

Captain Cook landed on Lizard Island in 1770, naming the island for its huge population of lizards, and climbed to the top of its granite mountain. From its summit, he was able to see a safe course out of the reef.

for many maps in use today. He warned others that they should come to the Great Barrier Reef only if they could "thread the needle . . . amongst the reef." Unable to follow his own advice, he lost his ship to the reef in 1803. He waited to be rescued for days on an unnamed island he called "a Small Uncertainty."

Following exploration, Queensland—one of Australia's five continental states—was first settled in 1824. It was used as a prison for the worst felons sent from Great Britain. In the 1890s, the Christian missions moved in. This finally resulted in the almost total devastation of the Aboriginal culture. In 1901, Australia became an independent nation— the Commonwealth of Australia. Development of the country began in earnest.

While settlement continued on the continent, others settled the reef islands. E. H. Banfield, an English-born journalist, settled on the uninhabited Dunk Island—largest of the sixteen Family Islands at the southern end of the reef—in 1897. Ordered by his physician to abandon the hectic life of a newspaperman, he and his wife explored many of the reef islands before choosing Dunk Island. Captain Cook had named the island earlier after the first lord of the admiralty. Dunk Island is the "father" of the family islands, while Bedarra, a short distance away, is the "mother."

Interest in the Great Barrier Reef continued. It was opened to detailed scientific research and com-

The reef was opened to both research and commerce in 1922. A turtle soup factory was started on Heron Island the next year. That factory was later converted to a tourist resort, saving the great turtles from the broth kettle.

Visitors to Green Island can see reef creatures from an underwater observatory.

merce about the same time. In 1922, the Great Barrier Reef Committee was established, to supervise marine research of the reef. Ironically, in 1923, a turtle soup cannery was opened on Heron Island. The committee established a very productive and famous research program on the Low Isles near the mouth of the Daintree River, under the direction of Sir Charles Maurice Yonge in 1928.

In his book *A Year on the Great Barrier Reef*, Yonge details the first major biological expedition to the Great Barrier Reef. He and his scientific colleagues lived on one of the two islands in the two-isle archipelago, a small, 3.5 acre (1.4 ha) cay, 185 yards (169 m) long and 110 yards (101 m) wide. They camped for a little over a year under a lighthouse.

The Great Barrier Marine Park was established in 1979, when a 4,556-square-mile (11,800-sq-km) area was set aside for the protection of the reef and its wildlife, and for tourists to visit. Tourists generally use the northern Queensland city of Cairns as their stepping-off point. Many take a boat to Green Island, which has an underwater observatory. Here visitors can observe life on the reef without even getting their feet wet. Corals, anemones, giant clams, and a host of other creatures perform their daily routines for the thousands who are curious to know about life under the sea.

Other visitors enjoy snorkeling or diving to view the underwater spectacle. Some people spend hours

Unique razor clams have narrow shells that look like sharp teeth. Their shells are usually only 8 inches (20 cm) in length.

Loggerhead turtles are protected within the boundaries of the Great Barrier Marine Park. The photo shows a female loggerhead turtle laying eggs.

exploring the shallow tidal pools—a very safe way to observe the reef. Tidal pools are found in a variety of shapes and sizes, and offer the careful observer a glimpse into an entire ecosystem that shimmers in crystal blue waters under a tropical sun.

The park shelters the largest breeding population of green sea turtles in the world. It also protects the largest population of loggerhead turtles in the Pacific Ocean area.

Pollution of Coral Reefs

Water and air circulate around the entire globe. Pollution in either of these natural resources can eventually affect the Great Barrier Reef and other coral reefs. The ecology of a coral reef is so fragile that minor changes in its environment can spell disaster for the reef and its inhabitants.

George Jones, the manager of John Pennekamp Coral Reef State Park, in Key Largo, Florida, was referring to the Southeast Florida Reef System, but his words apply equally to the Great Barrier Reef: "The quality of the water on the reef is just as important to the fish and coral there as the air we breathe is to us."

In 1975, the Australian federal government established the Great Barrier Marine Park Authority, which manages 98.5 percent, or 134,300 square miles (347,800 sq km), of the reef. Its slogan summarizes its main function of preserving and protecting it for the future—"Ours To Use Wisely."

The chances for survival of the reef were en-

"The Barrier Reef is a delicately balanced dynamic system, a self-fueled machine in which the sun's energy is converted into sea substances that become land-building materials. The reef environment is stable, but interference could disturb that stability. The reef machinery is fragile. If you damage it by dredging or quarrying or drilling or spilling oil, it may break down. Our technicians can only fix machines they build themselves. And this, the greatest creation of life on Earth, is no work of man."

— Dr. Patricia Mather, a scientist on the Great Barrier Reef Committee

hanced in 1981, when it was dedicated as a World Heritage Site. UNESCO acknowledged that it is the largest reef with the greatest species diversity. Residents of the reef include 1,500 different kinds of fish, 4,000 varieties of mollusks, and 400 types of hard and soft corals.

The world is changing rapidly, as the human population continues to grow and to put pressure on the environment. Our air is polluted by the technology developed by humans. Acid rain, caused by auto emissions and emissions from industry and power plants, could do great damage to the reef. If the ocean waters become more acidic, it may destroy life, as we know it, on the reef. Acid rain has already destroyed life in many lakes in Europe, the northeastern United States, and southeastern Canada.

Due to human population pressures, we are cutting down the forests of the world at rates much faster than they can replace themselves. Wood is needed by people for fuel, paper, and other products. The land is needed for farming, to feed all those people. As the forests are cut, much of the land is left barren, especially once it is discovered that it is not good for agriculture, or that it can be used only for a few years before the sparse nutrients are exhausted. This barren land is then subject to erosion by wind and also rain. Erosion sends millions of tons of soil into the rivers and, of course, into the oceans.

Thousands of unique species live in and around the Great Barrier Reef. Protecting the reef from pollution and damage should be of great concern.

In the oceans, this eroded soil usually settles to the bottom. Coral reefs cannot grow on soft, mucky bottoms. As the land erodes and creates more muck, which is deposited in the oceans, it limits the areas where coral reefs can grow and develop.

The chemistry of the ocean water itself is vital to maintaining a healthy reef system. Today, the Earth's waters are being polluted by mercury, polychlorinated biphenyls (PCBs) released by industrial processes, pesticides, oil spills, and who knows how many other toxic substances.

Each year more cruise ships bring more visitors to the Great Barrier Reef. Snorkeling is now a popular tourist activity.

For coral reefs, the chemical conditions of the water and surrounding environment are of extreme importance. Temperature is critical, as are light, salinity, and the nutrient and oxygen content of the water. Because reefs exist within such narrow environmental limits, they are susceptible to damage from slight changes in these conditions.

Too Many Visitors

The Great Barrier Reef must also be protected from the very people who love it. Because of its fragile ecological balance, it cannot handle an overload of visitors, picking and scraping souvenirs off its delicate surface.

The wildlife, too, must be protected. People must be prevented from overfishing and spearing on the reef. They must also not be permitted to remove live shells or coral. The reef's treasures are not inexhaustible. If everyone were allowed to pick away at it, eventually there would be nothing left. Even the most conscientious of visitors can, while clambering over the reef, unexpectedly break off chunks of growing coral, bringing to a halt the growth of that section of the reef.

What it all boils down to is that protection of the Great Barrier Reef is up to each individual person who visits the reef. People know the reef is protected by law, so now they must resist the temptation to collect its beautiful shells and coral.

The Future

Today, the reef must still be protected from modern technology and the development of the land and sea for people. With every passing year, the Earth finds itself deeper and deeper in an environmental crisis that may eventually destroy most of our natural world. As the human population continues to grow, added pressure will continue to be placed on Earth's natural resources and natural wonders.

Survival of the Great Barrier Reef and other reef systems in the world's oceans will depend on our ability to protect these wonders from exploitation and pollution. But, if human populations continue to grow at their present rate, none of Earth's resources will be safe from devastation.

Perhaps the best response to the present situation is education. If we inform people of the consequences of their actions and also expose them to the workings of nature and its fragility, then—maybe—changes will be made to insure the survival of Earth's resources.

Every day various species of plants and animals disappear from the face of the Earth. They cease to exist. It is estimated that by the end of this century over a million species living now will be extinct. Some of these extinctions are due to the activities of nature. At least four times in the evolutionary

A beautiful emperor angelfish glides through the Great Barrier Reef.

EXPLOITING THE REEF

One of the greatest dangers to the reef is exploitation by people. The silica sands that line the beaches of the Australian coast are valuable to industry. The calcium carbonate particles on the floor of the reef and on atolls and cays are also valuable to agriculture. These crystals could be used to reduce the acidity of soils. It is also suspected that there may be oil under the Great Barrier Reef.

What happens if we dredge the reef bottom for calcium, scoop up the sand off the beaches, and drill through the reef structure for oil? What took millions of years for nature to develop could be, within a matter of a few years, destroyed by people.

Exciting research is being done at the National Cancer Institute and other research facilities. Using sponges, sea squirts, and soft corals, all of which contain powerful toxic chemicals, experiments are being performed that show promise of improving the treatment of such human diseases as cancer, arthritis, and AIDS.

history of reefs, reef dwellers became nearly extinct on a large-scale basis, but they have always managed to rebuild themselves. Next time it may not be possible.

Today, people contribute to the evolutionary process of extinction. The activity of growing numbers of human beings the world over may spell the demise of the coral jungle off the coast of Australia.

In order to stop this destruction, we must do several things:

- Learn about the reef and how it functions. We need to know much more than we know today.

- Limit the activities of people on the reef. This will be a difficult task, since we must ask industries, governments, and pleasure-seekers to curtail certain activities. Any attempt to do this could be labeled as a "roadblock to progress." But block the road we must, if the reef is to survive.

- Prevent acid rain by reducing industrial pollution throughout the world. This will protect the reef while it protects all our water resources.

Can all this be done? The answer is yes. Today, some governments have taken steps to protect their countries'—and the world's—natural resources from the activities of people. We must push for more protection if we are to save the coral reefs from destruction in the future. Let's save this precious asset for future generations. A sustainable future for people and the Great Barrier Reef will benefit everyone.

Part of the reef near Lizard Island has been permanently destroyed by boat anchors. The delicate balance of every portion of the Great Barrier Reef must be protected from this type of careless destruction.

GLOSSARY

Aborigine – the first inhabitant of a country. Used primarily to describe precolonial tribal groups of Australia.

adaptation – a change in structure, function, or form that produces better adjustment of an animal or plant to its environment.

algae – a group of water plants, including seaweeds, that are one-celled, colonial, or many-celled, and which contain chlorophyll. These plants have no true root, stem, or leaf.

atoll – an oceanic reef that circles a lagoon.

barrier reef – a wall of coral that lies at the edge of a continental shelf. It separates the continental shelf from ocean waters.

bommie – a coral head rising straight up to within a yard or two of the water's surface.

budding – a method of reproduction, in which coral polyps produce exact copies of themselves. Budding polyps are always connected to one another and are constantly producing limestone to build the reef.

calcium carbonate ($CaCO_3$) – a chemical found in seawater and used by corals to build their skeletons; limestone.

carnivore – any animal that generally eats only flesh.

cay – an island formed when an outcrop of coral traps floating vegetation. Eventually it may support trees. Pronounced *kee*.

coelenterates – a group of animals that includes hard and soft corals, sea fans, hydras, and anemones. Also called cnidarians.

colony – a group of similar plants or animals living or growing together.

corallite – the limestone skeleton of each individual coral.

corallum – a colony of corallites growing together.

ecosystem – a specialized community, including all the component plants and animals, that forms an interacting system.

food chain – a sequence of organisms in a community, in which each member feeds on the next member in the chain.

fringing reef – a shelf reef that develops around oceanic islands, as well as on continental shelves.

glucose ($C_6H_{12}O_6$) – the sugar produced in the process of photosynthesis.

herbivore – any animal that eats primarily vegetation.

host – the animal preyed upon by a parasite.

larva – the newly hatched, earliest stage of the coral polyp. It floats freely in the sea.

limestone – a rock formed by the secretion of calcium carbonate by coral polyps.

mimicry – an adaptation, in which an animal is protected or able to find food because of the fact that it looks like a different animal. An example is the blenny fish.

niche – the role or place of an organism in its environment.

nutrient – any substance taken in by a plant or animal that is used in its metabolism.

oceanic reef – a reef located where the ocean floor rises to form submarine mountain ranges. Some of these mountains break the surface to form islands, and reefs form in the shallows of these islands.

omnivore – any animal that eats both animals and plants.

parasite – any organism that lives at the expense of another organism.

parasitism – a relationship in which one organism benefits and the other is harmed. The organism that benefits is called a parasite; the one harmed is called the host.

photosynthesis – the process by which green plants manufacture food. Plants use carbon dioxide, water, and light energy to produce glucose, a simple sugar, and oxygen, as a by-product.

plankton – the freely floating small plants and animals found in a body of water. Includes some algae, small crustaceans, jellyfish, and numerous microscopic creatures. Plankton serves as the main food of numerous larger creatures.

planula – the coral polyp's larva.

pollution – the contamination of air, water, or soil.

polyp – the actual coral animal that builds the reef, resembling a sea anemone. It is a carnivore that hunts mostly at night. The limestone material it leaves behind is its external skeleton.

predator – any animal that preys upon other animals for its food.

producer – any green plant; any organism that produces its own food; the base of the food chain.

protective coloration – an adaptation in which an animal takes on the color of its surroundings to hide itself.

shelf reef – a reef formed close to a continent, on its sloping shelf.

shoal – a shallow place in the water.

species – any group of animals capable of interbreeding, having common attributes, and assigned a common name.

structural adaptation – a unique structure which an animal possesses to help it survive in its environment.

zooplankton – the animals found in plankton.

zooxanthellae – algae that live and photosynthesize within the transparent cells of the coral polyp.

FOR MORE INFORMATION

Angel, Martin and Heather. *Ocean Life*. London: Octopus Books, 1974.

Blumberg, Rhoda. *The Remarkable Voyages of Captain Cook*. New York: Bradbury Press, 1991.

Burgess, Robert F. *Exploring a Coral Reef*. New York: Macmillan, 1972.

The Cousteau Society. *Corals: The Sea's Great Builders*. New York: Simon & Schuster, 1992.

Darwin, Charles. *Structure and Distribution of Coral Reefs*. New York: D. Appleton, 1901.

Gutnik, Martin J. *Ecology*. New York: Franklin Watts, 1984.

Hannan, Hano W. *In the Coral Reefs*. New York: Doubleday, 1974.

Idyll, C. P. *Abyss, the Deep Sea and the Creatures that Live in It*. New York: Thomas Y. Crowell, 1976.

MacLeish, Kenneth. "Exploring Australia's Coral Jungle." *National Geographic*, vol. 143, no. 6, June, 1973.

MacLeish, Kenneth. "Queensland." *National Geographic*, vol. 134, no. 5, November, 1968.

Nova. *City of Coral*. Video Classics.

Paige, David. *A Day in the Life of a Marine Biologist*. Mahwah, NJ: Troll, 1981.

Sheppard, Charles R. C. *A Natural History of the Coral Reef*. London: Blandford Press, 1983.

Starck, Walter A., II, Ph.D. "Marvels of a Coral Realm." *National Geographic*, vol. 130, no. 5, November, 1966.

Taylor, Ron and Valerie. "Paradise Beneath the Sea." *National Geographic*, vol. 159, no. 5, May, 1981.

Taylor, Ron and Valerie. "Australia's Great Barrier Reef." *National Geographic*, vol. 143, no. 6, June, 1973.

Veron, J.E.N. *Corals of Australia and the Indo-Pacific*. Sydney, Australia: Angus and Robertson, 1986.

Wood, Elizabeth M., Dr. *Corals of the World*. Neptune City, NJ: T. F. H. Publications, 1983.

Worrell, Eric. *The Great Barrier Reef*. Sydney, Australia: Angus & Robertson, 1966.

INDEX

ARDED

PEACHTREE

J 508.943 GUTNIK   PTREE   AUG 0 7 1998
Gutnik, Martin J.
Great Barrier Reef

Atlanta-Fulton Public Library